I0437480

Also by Elliott Perlin, M.D.

Like the Trailings of a Comet on an Endless Journey,
February, 2006, Infinity Publishing.com.

Breaking Addictions with Biblio/Poetry Therapy

Elliott Perlin, M.D.

authorHOUSE®

AuthorHouse™
1663 Liberty Drive
Bloomington, IN 47403
www.authorhouse.com
Phone: 1-800-839-8640

© 2009 Elliott Perlin, M.D.. All rights reserved.

No part of this book may be reproduced, stored in a retrieval system, or
transmitted by any means without the written permission of the author.

First published by AuthorHouse 5/18/2009

ISBN: 978-1-4389-7210-7 (sc)
ISBN: 978-1-4389-7211-4 (hc)

Printed in the United States of America
Bloomington, Indiana

This book is printed on acid-free paper.

This book is dedicated to all of those who
suffer from the illness of addiction.

The author thanks Varsha Morar, M.D.
for her excellent advice and encouragement.

He also thanks Amanda Kasper for her excellent
assistance in the preparation of this book.

PREFACE

In this excellently written book, Dr. Perlin takes us through an incredible emotional journey wherein the reader gains new insights and methods to assist in healing the suffering of those individuals with addictions. It is amazing that someone who is not in the mental health field would have such an enormous emotional intellect into this devastating mental illness and be able to utilize his longstanding love of poetry to assist in bringing about healing and change in those afflicted with one or more addictions.

With a well-informed background of addictions and biblio/poetry therapy, Dr. Perlin shares poems he has written on various addictions which enable the reader to have an emotional experience and gain deep insights into the various feelings that different addictions stir up. At the same time he often adds at the end a healing hope within them. For any professional or layperson this is a very easily readable and concise summary of the major addictions. It serves to remind us of the importance of the toll this illness has taken on thousands of individuals who are afflicted with an addiction.

I believe this book can definitely be used adjunctively by those therapists who work with patients who have addictions. By using this book, it will allow a therapist to be equipped with another tool at his or her disposal in their goal to bring about healing and change in others. It can also benefit those who are addicted as well as their families and friends.

In his last two poems at the end of the book Dr. Perlin shares with us a beautiful poem on positive addictions which allows one to connect on many positive levels and also removes the negative connotation to the word "addiction." In addition, the poem from a father to a son gives the reader heartfelt hope and empowers one to use this technique by envisioning change:

We never know what brings about change
Within individuals' brains
Yet we can be sure
That without endeavor
Life will truly not be better!!!

Being a child, adolescent and adult psychiatrist, I read this book thinking about how it could benefit my patients adjunctively with respect to the treatments already indicated in their specific mental illnesses. In addition, I saw that it could be beneficial to all of those who work with such individuals as a way of helping them to expand their emotional capacities and gain a greater depth of processing how patients really feel. For example, psychoanalysts who use verbal communication usually have to undergo psychoanalysis training and are more in touch with theirs and their patients' inner emotions; however, sometimes what a patient writes may very well be the repressed emotions that they could not express verbally within a session. Other professionals in the mental health field and also laypersons will benefit from this book as well. It is important to note that bibliotherapy includes both reading patients' materials as well as writing responses to them. Biblio/poetry therapy also includes spontaneous and well-thought-out written text in poetic, narrative or any other style.

There is a certain subset of patients that can only express their deepest inner feelings on paper. This exercise allows such patients to have a viable outlet for communicating and sharing their feelings with others. Healing may then occur as they realize that the feelings they have can be shared and appreciated by others. It is an alternative to alleviate the isolation felt by many individuals with mental and emotional illnesses, especially those with addictions. One of the reasons these individuals turn to addictions is that they see no other way out and have great difficulty in expressing their feelings of depression, anxiety and despair to others and become entrenched in a vicious internalized negative cycle.

These same individuals also are not always able to appreciate the significance of their emotions and inappropriate behavior. When they do become sober they are often anxious and/or depressed. The use of addicting substances is a way of suppressing these feelings. Healing can only come about when they become aware of their inner repressed feelings and gain an understanding of their behavior as they learn new ways of coping with life.

Varsha Morar, M.D.

CONTENTS

INTRODUCTION

When you wake up in the morning is your first thought: "I need a cup of coffee?" If so, then you are addicted to that first cup of coffee as many of us are. Addictions of all forms are ubiquitous. You need your coffee, your spouse may need his or her tea and the baby needs his or her bottle of milk.

Unfortunately, the "bottle" may contain something else in later years. Alcohol, nicotine, opioids, cocaine, steroids and other numerous drugs are addictive. In addition certain activities such as gambling, engaging in excessive sexual activity, eating too much or too little can also be addictive.

Even if we are addicted to that first cup of coffee in the morning or the Snickers bar (as I am) most of us can control our cravings.

Many others are not so fortunate. The statistics are astounding: there are about 190 million drug users throughout the world. There are 21 million who abuse cocaine or heroin, 140 million who consume marijuana and hashish, 30 million who abuse synthetic stimulants. In the US alone, 13.8 million people are alcoholics; 43% of American adults have a child, parent, sibling, or spouse who is an alcoholic (World Drug Report, Oxford University Press, 1997).

The purpose of this book is to introduce the therapeutic value of what some call "bibliotherapy" (which includes "poetry therapy" as part of its definition) with respect to addictions. Its basis is that the origins of addictions, notwithstanding the complexity of their background, derive from subconscious disturbances that result from a genetic propensity and/or adverse life experiences.

Thus exploring the unconscious mind with this tool in order to expose the underlying conflict or conflicts may allow an individual to understand and control his or her addictions. In a way it is therefore an adjunct of psychotherapy.

In this book I will discuss briefly the various common addictions, highlighting only their key features. Other therapy is not addressed. (This information can be found in other sources.) Each section is introduced with a poem. These poems are not intended to be masterpieces of poetic expression, but rather emphasize the dangers of the addictive substances. Some are purposely written in a somewhat humorous or semi-humorous style to attract the reader's attention. They can be used to assist in initiating a therapeutic dialogue during individual or group therapy. They can also be used as models or stimulation to help enable patients asked or encouraged to produce their own poetry or a narrative exposition. In short they are "food for thought". I want to emphasize that they are not meant to ridicule or embarrass the addicted individual.

You might ask, "Why did I write this book". I am not a psychologist or psychiatrist, but a hematologist/oncologist with over forty years of experience caring for patients with blood disorders and cancer. These illnesses often carry an association with depression, anxiety, loss of self-esteem, etc. I realized that patients with life-threatening diseases, like individuals with psychiatric illnesses, need help with regard to the psychological aspects of their sickness. I have also cared for many patients with sickle cell disease, a chronic blood disease associated with anemia and other manifestations. This disease also requires psychological support. Therefore part of my ministering to patients with cancer and blood diseases required a certain amount of psychotherapy. Thus my patients and others with similar chronic illnesses may also benefit from biblio/poetry therapy.

Also you may wonder what experience I have regarding the reading and writing of poetry. I have enjoyed reading poetry for many years and I have been writing poetry for over 20 years. My work has been published in professional journals, such as, *The Annals of Internal Medicine, The Pharos, Perspectives in Biology and Medicine*, periodicals, various newspapers and elsewhere. I have also published a book of poetry, "Like the Trailings of a Comet on an Endless Journey" (2006)

(Infinity Publishing.com). This book of poetry tracks my life from boyhood to my professional experiences and contains many poems related to my patients. I have also written close to 100 professional scientific articles.

Finally, and most importantly, for whom is this book written? It is intended to introduce this form of therapy to those of the medical profession who are unfamiliar with it (as I was before learning of its existence), therapists who treat addicts (i.e., professionals and their allied workers such as those who lead AA and similar meetings regarding other addictions); and specialty physicians who deal with patients who have chronic or fatal illnesses and require improvement of their coping skills; all those interested in learning new things; and most especially addicts themselves who have never heard of this therapy and are looking for another pathway to conquer their illness.

It should be emphasized that this form of therapy is only adjunct to other more conventional therapy. Also it will only be of value when the individual afflicted has a strong desire to understand his or her illness and uses biblio/poetry therapy to probe the deeper parts of the brain. Used in this way it is therefore a tool of psychotherapy and/or psychoanalysis.

How can literature or creative writing help people to heal? When you first think about it does seem absurd when one considers that creative writing includes poetry, novels, short stories, plays, operas and other forms of entertainment. All of these represent aspects of life, including the utilization of our senses, various life crises, humorous and sad events, times of war and peace, visiting various places in the world, etc.

However, let's look at poetry for a moment. Poetry can be a median of self-expression wherein our deepest feelings and emotions are expressed. For example, we can use poetry to represent love, hate, anger, grief, and many other human emotions and thoughts. The careful reader of a poem can often connect with its representations sufficiently to evoke an awakening of subconscious thoughts and memories related to his or her life. Pondering on these thoughts may evoke actions leading to a change in one's life and for an addict becoming mentally well.

But can poetry really serve as a therapeutic tool? In the *American Medical News*, May 17, 1999, Deborah L. Shelton tells us that the "marriage of poetry and medicine goes way back. In ancient Egypt sacred words were chanted in rituals to promote healing... Even in the modern era poetry has played a role. The famed Benjamin Rush, M.D., included a library in the hospital he founded in 1810 so patients could read poetry and other literature prescribed by their doctors. Many notable poets were also physicians, including William Carlos Williams, Anton Checkhov, John Keats and Oliver Wendell Holmes..."

Many psychiatrists and psychologists may use biblio/poetry therapy to help patients crystallize his or her feelings in words that reflect the mental disturbance affecting them. "It's the process not the final product that matters." "It's the way a patient tells the most things about his or her life," says John Stone, M.D. a Professor of Medicine at Emory University. Thus the dialogue between a patient and his or her therapist can be considered poetic expression.

The broader terms "bibliotherapy or biblio-poetry therapy" extend "literary therapy" to more than simply verse. It can include many forms of literature such as short stories, fables, myths, memoirs, and journal entries. Thus the more comprehensive term "bibliotherapy" is probably its best descriptor of this form of therapy.

In the *Journal of Poetry Therapy* vol. 10, No. 3, 1997, Sherry Reiter, CSW, PTR, RDT states that poetry therapy and biblio-therapy is the use of literature for the process of healing and personal growth. The concept of "catharsis" is a release of thoughts, concerns and worries through spontaneous "free thought" (compare with the term "free verse"). Creative writing of all types represents a form of catharsis for the writer who hopes it will similarly emotionally affect the reader (in some way) as well.

Sherry Reiter lists the purposes of biblio/poetry therapy as follows:
1. To enhance self-understanding and accuracy in self-perception;
2. To increase awareness of interpersonal relationships;
3. To heighten reality orientation;
4. To help develop creativity, self-expression and greater self-esteem;
5. To encourage positive thinking and creative problem solving;
6. To strengthen communication (particularly listening and speaking skills);
7. To integrate the different aspects of the self for psychological wholeness;

8. To ventilate overpowering emotions and release tension;
9. To find new meaning through new ideas, insights and/or information; and
10. To help participants experience the liberating and nourishing qualities of beauty.

So how does biblio/poetry therapy work? Firstly, it requires a trained biblio/poetry therapist who may select a published poem or excerpt from prose which may serve as a "catalyst" or "stimulator" of emotional feeling. The main goal of this exercise is to evoke a reaction to the piece selected. A spontaneous emotional response is encouraged; it is hoped that an expression of anger, anxiety, depression and/or other emotions occur. If this does not happen the client(s) is (are) prompted to express (his, her, their) feelings regarding the selection and asked to attempt to relate these feelings to their own psychiatric or psychological problem(s) (which could be one or more addictions). Examples of a "catalyst" selection that a poetry therapist might use are these words written by the poet James Kevanaugh:

I laugh and cry with the same eyes
Love and hate with the same heart
I feel my rage and my gentleness

or these lines written by Alice Walker:

How I miss my father;
I wish he had not been
so tired
when I was born

The selection could also be a complete poem or prose selection as well.

The biblio-poetry therapy session can take place in the setting of individual or group therapy. There are three stages in the interactive process:
1. Recognition of the selection (the author, the main content, purpose of the poem, etc.);
2. Reactions to the poem or narrative or parts of it; and
3. "Juxtaposition"- applying the poem to the patients' problems.

A good example of the interactive process could be a discussion of Robert Frost's poem "The Road Not Taken" (see the Introduction to Part V). ("Which road would you have taken and why?")

There is also a form of poetry therapy that is called "soulspeak". It is an ancient (tribal) form of poetry that creates a simple poem that can be put to music if desired. Two people may participate in the exercise creating a story, lyrics for a song, or simply a narrative that is intended to be evoked from the "deepest" part of a man or woman (i.e., his or her "soul") where the most intense emotions arise from a human being. The words therefore are to be derived from the "unconscious", "spiritual", or "soul" area of the brain. Here is an example of such an exercise:

Patient: I wish I had a bottle of scotch right now

Therapist: Suppose I get it for you

Patient: Really, that's great!

Therapist: I changed my mind; it's bad for you

Patient: Oh... why?

Therapist: It can be poison; it can kill you!

Patient: Oh, yea

Thus, in summary, biblio-poetry therapy (and its broader terms bibliotherapy or literary therapy) is therapy that uses the tool of creative writing (both published works and the writings of clients and therapists) to assist those individuals who are mentally troubled to enhance an understanding of their illnesses and themselves. It can be used in all settings where psychotherapy takes place, i.e., doctors offices, psychiatric units (inpatient and outpatient), community health centers, chemical dependency groups (eg., "AA") and various other settings.

There is an organization known as the National Association for Poetry Therapy (NAPT) that supports this form of therapy by setting up standards of practice, ethical codes, training requirements, and defining the body of knowledge that is essential for the utilization of this therapeutic tool. It also publishes a newsletter and *The Journal of Poetry Therapy*. It is also the sponsor of a four day yearly national conference. There are a number of other similar national and local organizations as well.

NAPT believes that the benefit of biblio-poetry therapy need not be limited to mental illnesses. It can be applied to a wide variety of social and medical problems. These could include soldiers under constant stress, adolescents having problems socializing or experiencing school difficulties, prisoners attempting to become rehabilitated, seniors undergoing a difficult time adjusting to old age, the physically challenged and survivors of injury, abuse, violence, rape and other "life shaking" experiences as well as a host of chronic medical conditions that can be accompanied with mental stress.

The goals of NAPT relative to the patient or client are listed as follows:

1. To develop creativity, self expression and greater self-esteem;
2. To strengthen interpersonal and communication skills;
3. To provide a medium wherein afflicted individuals can ventilate their emotions and release tension;
4. To allow the finding of a new meaning of the individuals' emotions and feelings via the accrual of new fresh ideas, insights and learning; and
5. Help promote the enhancement of coping skills and the ability to adapt to adverse conditions.

The format of this book is as follows: In Part I (The Addictions) an addiction is introduced with a poem, then the addiction itself is briefly described. Standard medical treatment is not addressed since this information can be obtained from other multiple sources.

Part II describes how biblio-poetry can be used as a therapeutic tool. The last 20 years of *The Journal of Poetry Therapy*, edited by Nicholas Mazza is used as a backbone for this section.

Finally, Part III discusses more specifically how biblio/poetry can help the addicted individual using examples from the literature.

The book also contains a glossary of terms frequently found in *The Journal of Poetry Therapy* and a short list of pertinent references for further reading. It concludes with a poem listing those "addictions" that are "good to have" and also a poem written by a father to a son, which could represent poetry therapy for both.

PART I

THE ADDICTIONS

ALCOHOLISM

A Prayer for the Alcoholic

Dear G-d:

Please give me back
my sobriety; please
propel me back
to society.

Please help me
not to fall
ever again to alcohol.

Please free me
from that evil
that threw my life
into upheaval!

Please, please
set me free--
So that once again
I can know myself-
and my family
and friends
can know me!

ALCOHOLISM

Alcoholism is a major health problem in the United States and around the world. Men often in their prime years are affected more often than women by about 5 to 1. The cause of alcoholism is not known, but many people turn to alcohol to alleviate their depression, tensions, frustrations and/or anxieties. Of course when individuals so afflicted become sober, they find themselves more mentally ill than before the alcoholic binge and are unable to function effectively.

Alcohol is a depressant itself and can cause serious and irreversible physical damage to the brain, liver and other parts of the body when used in excess. Continuous abuse of alcohol can lead to neurological illnesses such as delirium tremens and Korsakoff's psychosis. Damage to the liver may lead to a condition known as cirrhosis which can lead to an early death. Social failure with respect to marriage, parenthood and employment frequently ensues, leading to isolation, loss of income, destitution, and even incarceration.

ANOREXIA

KATEY THE ANOREXIC

Katey was an anorexic--
she preferred to be cachectic;

Her joy was in "not in eatin";
she liked to get her "dopamine
secretin';

Pushing away her plate of food
put her in a cheery mood!

But by and by she lost so
much weight
she began to worry about her fate;

Realizing she had made a big mistake
she cooked herself a 3 pound steak!

ANOREXIA
("*Starvation Addiction*")

Strange as it may seem, anorexia nervosa results from an "addiction to dieting". Some people feel good when they are dieting. The effect of dieting simulates the mechanism of action of the drug known as ecstasy which also suppresses appetite according to an article which recently appeared in the magazine <u>Scientific American Mind</u> (June 12, 2008). Anorexics seem to prefer "living for the future" but often die at a young age. The exact pathophysiology of the disorder is not completely understood but a genetic defect may be the driving force. Some anorexics, like Katey, eventually realize the folly of their addiction.

BARBITURATES

DON'T GET STUCK WITH A BARB

Barbital is **not** what you've heard;
Please, my friend, take me at my word;

Don't think at all
That you can't croak
From abusing barbital!

Withdrawal is dangerous too-
That process has killed
More than a few!

So, my friend, before **you** fall--
Give up that "trip" with barbital!

BARBITURATES

There are many sedatives that have been abused. The barbiturates are only one of them. Others include meprobamate, amobarbital, benzodiazepines, and many more new ones, eg., Ambien.

All of these drugs except meprobamate work through a substance known as gamma-aminobutyric acid (also known as GABA) which depresses brain cells causing lethargy and sleepiness. The danger is that they can cause (in excessive doses) respiratory and cardiac depression. Withdrawal from these drugs can also be dangerous, leading to convulsions and hyperthermia. Delirium and hallucinations can also occur. A significant mortality rate of up to 20% exists from withdrawal from barbiturates.

BENZODIAZEPINES

A "Benzo" Can Turn You Into a "Bozo"
(The Story of an Ativan Abuser)

Once a fine young fellow
thought he was quite mellow, saying:
 "I'm as calm as a clam
I am, I am".

But on one school day, 'fore taking a test
(one that required his very best),
'e became nervously ill,
decided to swallow a pill,
becoming a fan of
Ativan.

'e was fine for a while
and continued to smile,
saying again "I'm as calm as a clam
I am, I am".

But bye and bye on this ride
'e became suddenly manic,
overdosed 'is Ativan in a panic
and had to be detoxified.

'e was then fathered and mothered
and eventually recovered
and again said:
"I'm as calm as a clam
I am, I am"

Confessed he:
I'm sorry I fell
into the arms of hell!
And I thank G-d I survived
this unfortunate ride-
I was so sick
I almost died!

And 'e promised never again
to be
a fan of Ativan!

BENZODIAZEPINES

These drugs, thought of as "modern tranquilizers," are frequently prescribed for psychiatric illnesses and medical conditions associated with anxiety. They have largely supplanted the previously popular drugs like meprobamate, chlordiazepoxide (Librium) and others.

They are quite safe if used conservatively for relatively short periods of time. However, if they are used with alcohol and other sedative-type drugs, they can be dangerous causing over sedation and possibly respiratory depression. If they are used for long periods of time, they can cause headaches, visual disturbances, anxiety, agitation, rashes, loss of bladder control and interference with the menstrual cycle.

COCAINE

COCAINE

Drug Pusher:

"Hey, man, got some stuff-
It's pretty tough—
Want a puff?

It's "crack" you know—
Born 3000 years ago—
Some call it coke or snow—

In just 10 seconds you are high—
It'll make you laugh or cry..."

****

Previous Cocaine Addict:

"No thanks, man, my mind's been blown—
My pulse was fast, blood pressure high—
Surely didn't want to die—
That "bad boy" had found my head—
Thought I: Not long 'fore I'll be dead
or at least have a stroke
from snortin' th' stuff called coke...

****

Man, we have a choice
before we hear our Maker's voice—

Let it go, my friend, let it go,
Let that "bad boy" go...."

COCAINE

Cocaine is a very popular drug of abuse. It comes in four different preparations: a powder, a paste and two solid forms. The drug is derived from the coca plant. From its natural presentation as coca paste, it can be extracted with ether and converted to a powder (cocaine hydrochloride) which can be snorted, generating in a user what is known as a "rush".

"Freebase" and "crack cocaine" are derived from cocaine hydrochloride also. The former is a direct derivative of cocaine hydrochloride; crack cocaine is derived from its extraction with baking soda.

Base forms are swallowed alone or with heroin (the combination is sometime called a "boy-girl") or with the drug phencyclidine (also known by some as "space-base"). These "base forms" of cocaine are more addicting because they reach the brain more quickly.

A metabolite of cocaine can be detected in the urine. The drug has an interesting history. It was first used by pre-Columbian civilizations in South America 3000-4000 years ago. In the Napoleonic period it was employed as both a medical and recreational drug.

The drug works by releasing the neurotransmitter called "dopamine", which produces a euphoric state. In time, with continued use, dopamine becomes depleted and the individual feels the need to replace it with more cocaine.

Many adverse medical events can result with the use of cocaine, such as infections from sharing needles, damage to the nasal tissue from snorting it, and cardiac injury. Pregnant mothers who use it may experience spontaneous abortions. Also babies born to them (known as "crack babies") may be smaller than normal, hyperactive, and have poor coordination.

Several drugs are now being studied to treat cocaine addiction (see Scientific American Mind, April/May 2008).

COMPULSIVE GAMBLING

GAMBLING

The Gambler: "You gotta know when to hold 'em…"

Friend: "You'd be better off to fold 'em!"

The Gambler: OK, I'll just roll these dice- my baby needs new shoes; I know I can't lose, I'll throw only fives and twos!

Friend: No, not the way to go- Come on with me-- let's blow!

The Gambler: First let's go to the track–won't be long 'fore we're back; I know all 'bout horses- We'll win big with my choices!

Friend: No! Not good to bet on ponies; those who say otherwise are phonies! Let's pack it up, go home-- STAT. We'll be better off--you can bet on that!!

COMPULSIVE GAMBLING

Do you like to play the slot machines? Play poker? Bet on the horses? Or have other gambling habits? We all enjoy gambling to some extent, but when it becomes a compulsion, it is a disease that you want to avoid.

The concept of gambling of various types has been around for many years, probably starting in China about 2300 B.C. Card playing may have started there too but the French were responsible for creating our current 52 card deck.

Card playing, as we know it today, started with the games blackjack and poker in China about 900 A.D. Roulette (meaning "small wheel" in French) began in France. Some believe that the mathematician Blaine Pascal created the wheel.

Race tracks, casinos and numerous private card parties give credence to the fact that many people like to gamble for recreation. However, when it becomes a compulsive habit, it is an illness. The compulsive gambler may ignore his family as well as personal and business responsibilities. He or she may even turn to crime to support gambling habits.

At present, it is estimated that about 15 million people may be compulsive gamblers in the USA. There are many warning signs that you may be a compulsive gambler, such as an inability to stop your gambling activity whether winning or losing, neglecting your personal responsibilities to gamble, using gambling to relieve your depression, etc.

FOOD ADDICTION

THE "TRUE" STORY OF JACK SPRATT
(Indeed, he did eat fat!)

Jack Spratt, the food addict,
ate two pounds of haddock,
then downed a dozen eggs,
finishing this tasty meal
with six chicken legs!

He followed this
with some tuna fish,
then chug-a-lugged three pints of beer,
while those of us looking on
thought it very queer!

For his desert
'e thought it wouldn't hurt
to consume three apple pies-
they went down quick, didn't make 'im sick
which was much to our surprise!

When asked, without bein' rude,
Jack, how is it you c'n eat so much food?
'e simply answered "Hey! What's a stomach for?"
'n now I'm itchin to go into th' kitchen
So I can eat some more!"

FOOD ADDICTION

Everyone knows that there is an epidemic of obesity in the United States. It is one of the conditions that has reduced the United States' standing in comparative world health statistics. Why is this? Certainly, a genetic disposition exists that apparently is a dominant genetic characteristic in many families. In addition, the popularity of "fast food" restaurants that attract thousands of Americans every day also contributes to our overweight population.

On the other hand, there is such an illness known as "food addiction". This can be defined as compulsive craving for food despite the fact that you may not actually feel hunger associated with this craving. Also there is a tendency for food addicts to eat foods that may be harmful, such as foods with a high carbohydrate or fat content.

Those who have this addiction would answer "yes" to the following questions:
1. Do you eat even if you are not hungry?
2. Do you eat when you feel sad or depressed?
3. Do you tend to eat by yourself because you don't want others to see you eating?
4. Do you eat until you are "stuffed" and then feel that you need to "purge" afterward by inducing vomiting and/or using laxatives?
5. Does eating make you feel guilty?

Interestingly, not all food addicts are obese. And conversely, all obese individuals are not food addicts. There is no "typical" food addict. The illness can occur in the young, old, the overweight, underweight and those of normal weight.

HEROIN

Heroin Ain't No Heroine

Henry liked to "snort" his "stuff";
said it makes him really tough;

Susie prefers to shoot it in; she
likes the way it "pops" her skin;

Bobby prefers "chasin' the dragon";
that really gets his tail waggin'!

Hey, doesn't matter how goes in the "poppy"—
bye and bye you're feelin' hoppy!

****

Said the "pusher":

Hey, man, want a puff?
This is it- the real good stuff!

Sure do, says you!

Yeh, but next you know yer feeder's gone—
Musta went outa town—
There ain't no more skag around!

I'll kick the habit so you say—
Man… just ain't 'n easy way…

Y'r BP's high, pulse iz up,
Y'r one hell-a-va sick pup!

Y'r hot, y'r cold, y'r skin is wet,
y'r muscles 'r twitchin' 'n you start bitchin'

Hell..p! ya yelp, but no one's 'round,
I'm losin' it man, I'm goin' down!

But just then
yr clean buddy appears—
He's all eyes, yr all ears...

Hey, man, yr the one who let the terror in—
Don't ya know—
Heroin's a bad girl—it ain't no heroine!

Opioid Addictions

Opioids consist of a large group of drugs that include both natural and synthetic substances. The drugs are derived from the opium poppy grown in a number of areas of the world, eg., Southwest Asia (the golden crust of Afghanistan), Pakistan, Iran, Southeast Asia (Laos, Thailand and Barona), Mexico and Columbia. Opioids are used medically primarily to relieve pain, but also can function as cough suppressants and antidiarrheal agents. They include codeine, oxycodone, meperidine, fentanyl, hydromorphine, methadone, propoxyphene, and heroin. The latter drug is not usually used medically because it is very addicting. It was brought to our country by Chinese immigrants in the late 1880's; many opiates were easily available at that time in the western part of the country. Heroin can be injected (intravenously or under the skin), but can also be smoked or "snorted" intranasally.

The use of heroin (and other opiates less so) result in a "high"- i.e., a euphoric state of being. However, drowsiness, slurred speech, and a lack of sensitivity to pain also ensue. Dependence on these drugs occurs quickly.

The dependency on opioids is both physiological and psychological. It becomes very difficult for an individual to give up opioids (especially heroin) once exposed to them. Tolerance builds up rapidly. If the individual chooses to withdraw from opiates major symptoms occur such as a fast pulse, high blood pressure, sweating, muscle pain, fearfulness, and other unpleasant symptoms.

KHAT

Beware of the Khat

In some countries
it's legal to
chew some khat.

The leaves are tasty
and won't make you fat.

And by and by
you'll feel as high
as a kite
and really believe
that you're "all right".

But wait, before
you take that ride
better know the other side.

It can leave you
"hanging", confused
and agitated-
O yes, this khat is overrated!

Hey, man, forget it—
I mean right now—
khat really ain't
the "cat's meow"!

KHAT

Many people never heard of the Khat bush but it is the largest source of a natural stimulant extract in the world. Scientifically called *catha edulis*, it has been used by many people in the Middle East for a long time. Even devout Muslims may use it in lieu of alcohol.

The active ingredient in this plant is called cathinone, a stimulant substance similar to amphetamine. The leaves are chewed within three days after being picked from the plant. Short term abuse is like taking a drink or two of an alcoholic beverage; it can result in increased socialization and sexuality. However, like amphetamines, it can increase blood pressure and heart rate. Prolonged use increases thirst and causes polyuria (increased urination).

Daily chewing of the leaves can lead to an altered mental state with variable features such as anxiety, agitation, confusion, and even a psychotic state of mind.

MARIJUANA

WANNA SMOKE SOME MARIJUANA?

Go ahead, smoke it
by itself…
it's right there
on the kitchen shelf!

Rather mix it
with cocaine or lime?
You're sure to have
a glorious time!

And brewed in tea
with a bit of catnip
will give you
quite a pleasant trip!

But marijuana
isn't all fun—
Oh no, this poem
isn't yet done.

Sooner or later
you will crash
from smoking that
stuff called hash.

This verse intends
to make the point…

…Hey!
"you really don't
wanna smoke
that joint!!"

Marijuana

Marijuana has the distinction of being the most abused drug throughout the world. Amazingly, it contains 400 ingredients but the most potent one is tetrahydrocannibol. Abusers smoke it alone or along with other substances such as phencyclidine, crack cocaine, and mineral lime. It was first used in China about 1000 years B.C. and introduced to the western hemisphere about 1500 A.D. Physicians employed it as a medicine in the early 1800's as an analgesic, anticonvulsant and muscle relaxant.

Marijuana can impair memory caused by the stimulation of dopamine production. It can also interfere with balance, decrease blood pressure and speed up the heart. It also may increase the risk of lung infections, cause atrophy of the testes and stimulate breast enlargement. Depression is also common.

PSYCHEDELICS

LARRY LIKED LSD
(*Unfortunately*)

Larry just loved to party
at gatherings especially naughty;

You see he had a craving for LSD,
claiming: "Hey, it makes my mind run free!"

He saw colors-- green, blue and brown
and became enchanted when the room went round...

But then one day he got such a buzz
that he didn't know where he was!

His head hurt, his feet felt like lead--
and (O my!) a little later
he was dead!

PSYCHEDELICS

Psychedelics, also known as "hallucinogens", are not in use as much these days. Their history, however, is very interesting. They may have first been used over 3,000 years ago from an extract from a poison mushroom known as fly agaric. Later a plant parasite living on rye stalks produced a psychedelic known as ergot alkaloid. Modern psychedelics appeared when Albert Hofmann at Sandoz Laboratories in Switzerland synthesized D-lysergic acid diethylamide-25 (LSD) in the 1930's. In the 1960's Merck Pharmaceuticals produced "Ecstasy" which was legalized for use by psychiatrists to relax their patients and encourage openness during therapeutic sessions. However, the FDA, eventually realizing the potential danger of this class of drugs cancelled its legalization.

Psychedelics can cause hallucinations and various sensory distortions. LSD can also cause "synesthesia", a peculiar merging of the senses (like taste and smell). It can also cause an enhancement of color.

The abuse of LSD is extremely dangerous and can cause death.

PHENCYCLIDINE

DISSOCIATIVES CAN UNCOUPLE YOU

Phencyclidine, thought to be keen,
acts a lot like an amphetamine;

But at times it'll fool ya—
calm ya down an' then cool ya;

Abused by Haight-Ashbury folks in '67,
they thought the drug was sent from heaven;

The drug was composed by chemists for hire
who developed it from platinum wire!

Its use has led to many crimes-
the felons jailed or slapped with fines;

Once known as "mad hatter" or "dry as a bone"... forget it!
It's best to leave phencyclidine alone!!

PHENCYCLIDINE

Phencyclidine (also known as PCP) is what some call a "dissociative" because it "dissociates" one from reality. It is often combined with other drugs of abuse such as amphetamine and marijuana. It can cause symptoms of hypersexuality, hyperaggressiveness, and loss of appetite.

It was first reported to be a drug of abuse in the Haight-Ashbury district of San Francisco back in 1967 where it was called the "peace pill".

It became under scrutiny when it began to become associated with crime, self-disfigurement and even suicide.

It can be taken as a pill, snorted up the nose, inhaled as a liquid, or smoked. Long term use can result in depression. Children born to mothers who use it may have an increased startle reflux, spasticity and tremor.

STEROIDS

What Was the Real Reason the Mighty Casey Struck Out?

(*With apologies to Ernest Lawrence Thayer*)

Casey was a baseball star;
he could hit a baseball really far;
watching 'im bat was quite a treat;
'e always got the crowd on its feet!

One day with the game on the line,
the fans havin' one fine time,
Casey stood 'n grabbed 'is bat,
then turned to the crowd n' tipped 'is hat;
he stared at the pitcher with a wicked grin,
thinking, "I'll hit a homer and our team will win!"

The first pitch was thrown over plate,
but Casey's swing was a little late!

Stee-rike one, the umpire called;

the next pitch seemed close inside,
so Casey thought: "I'll let it ride!"

Stee-rike two, screeched the umpire;

Casey smiled and dug in, ready to go!
'e stared at the pitcher
who was movin' slow;
then the pitcher took 'is wind up and
'is pitch came in with a zing!
The mighty Casey took a giant swing!

Stee-rike three!

Let lose the crowd moans and groans while wondering:
"Did Casey
forget to take his steroid hormones??"

STEROID ABUSE

Abuse of steroids has recently received a great deal of media attention. Athletes in all sports seeking an enhanced physical capability (completely ignoring the adverse effects of these dangerous drugs) are the largest population affected. Steroids have a negative effect on the heart, liver, sexual organs, endocrine glands, the immune system, the skin, bones and brain. They can increase "bad" cholesterol (LDL cholesterol) and triglycerides, cause hypertension, and accelerate arteriosclerotic heart disease; they can cause elevation of liver enzymes and even induce liver tumors; acne can appear; increases in sugar and altered pituitary hormone production can occur; tendon degeneration and premature epiphyseal closure of joints may take place; and finally they can dangerously cause personality changes that lead to violence and self-destruction.

Other hormones and substances that have been used to enhance physical performance are testosterone precursors, human growth hormone, creatinine, ephedra, erythropoietin and various herbal substances.

SYMPATHOMIMETICS

AMPHETAMINE CAN BE MEAN

Lizzy downed an "upper"
just before her supper
then jabbered through the meal;
On she babbled, becoming unraveled;

Asked her Dad:
"What's the matter?
Why the chatter?
How do you feel?"

Said Lizzy,
I feel fine,
just drank some wine,
so what's the big deal?

****

But Dad later learned
that she'd been burned
from a dose of amphetamine!

AMPHETAMINES

Amphetamines are in the family of drugs known as sympathomimetics. They are known on the street as "uppers". There are quite a few drugs that fall into this class, many of them legal. This makes it fairly easy to obtain possession of them.

An occasional user experiences the major effects of shakiness, dilated pupils, rapid heart beat, and a high energy level. Chronic abusers may feel panicky, frightened or depressed. Fever, rapid breathing and an impaired gait can occur.

TOBACCO

SMOKE, SMOKE THAT CIGARETTE...

"Til you smoke yr'self to death,"
and never take another breath;
it won't be long 'for yr hackin'
from those cigarettes yr packin'-
they're bad, they're mean,
full of tar and nicotine!

****

"But I like t' smoke", you answer
Hey, don't ya know they'll give ya cancer?
...that with every pack
y'r closer to a heart attack?
They kill yr lungs, can cause a stroke
Man, what I'm sayin' ain't no joke!
So give 'em up now...
'fore yr croakin'!
Ya just gotta get smart 'n stop yr smokin'!

TOBACCO

Tobacco has been in use for over 2000 years BC, first used by Native Americans in North and South America. Christopher Columbus brought tobacco back to Spain and from there it spread to the rest of the world via trade routes. It is processed from the fresh leaves of the plant called *Nicotiana.* Smoking tobacco is ubiquitous throughout the world in the form of cigarettes, cigars, pipes (straight or via the hookah) and chewing tobacco.

Tobacco smoke contains both nicotine and a monoamine oxidant inhibitor (preventing the breakdown of compounds containing a nitrogen element) called "harmane". The result of starting smoking initially may increase alertness and memory and produce mild euphoria. But nicotine can also reduce appetite and increase blood sugar levels.

Nicotine also can raise the blood pressure and heart rate. Tobacco smoke generates carbon monoxide, reducing oxygen availability. Carbon monoxide can also cause damage to the inside of the blood vessels. It is well known that the impurities in tobacco cause cancer of the upper airways and lung and emphysema (a chronic lung disease that is associated with damage to the air sacs (alveoli)). The use of tobacco killed 100 million people in the 20th century and may kill many more than this in the 21st century.

Passively inhaling smoke is also harmful and can result in asthma, upper respiratory infections, heart attacks and even "sudden death syndrome" in infants. It may also cause mood disorders, anxiety and depression.

Unfortunately, its danger has been ignored by many very intelligent people who apparently do not fear playing Russian roulette with their lives.

Tobacco companies have enhanced the danger by their super productive and false advertisements.

PART II

THERAPEUTIC APPLICATIONS OF BIBLIO/POETRY THERAPY

(A Look at the *Journal of Poetry Therapy* and a Discussion of the Value of Biblio/Poetry Therapy)

How can poetry (or prose) be employed as a therapeutic tool? *The Journal of Poetry Therapy* (JPT) has been publishing scholarly articles in the academic area of the practice of poetry therapy for 20 years. In June 2008 the collected abstracts of JPT were published by its editor Nicholas Mazza, PhD., of Florida State University. The first volume of the journal was published in the fall of 1987.

The lead article of JPT by Helen Jaskoski spoke of poetry writing in general being either "object-centered" or "process-centered," in other words in a way being "descriptive" or "interpretive". Perhaps the best poems combine these approaches. Subsequent articles apply poetry therapy to a wide range of medical and psychiatric conditions.

Special populations thought to be ideal for the applications of biblio/poetry therapy are the depressed elderly, trauma victims, sexually abused women, the incarcerated, some schizophrenics, some individuals who are mentally retarded, trauma victims, patients with AIDS and other chronic illnesses, soldiers returning from combat and teenagers with social and self-identity problems, and the target population of this book, those with various addictions.

A paper in the JPT in the winter of 1990 issue (pp. 71-81) by Helene McCarty Hynes entitled "Poetry: An Avenue into the Spirit" developed a compendium of the goals of biblio/poetry therapy using the acrostic "S-P-I-R-I-T," representing Spirituality, Perception, Insight, Relevancy, Integration, and Totality. In other words biblio/poetry therapy affects one's **spirit** (i.e., one's "feelings") and **perception**, one's **understanding** and/or **insight** of the **relevant** problem(s) in focus, how the poem **integrates** itself into the illness's solution(s), and finally how the poem can reconstruct one's "**totality**", i.e. one's "wholeness" as a person.

An article to help family members communicate more effectively with an addicted member is a study by J. Daniels, entitled "Father and Son: Using the Poetic to Enhance Communication" (JPT, Spring 1995, pp. 195-208).

Environmental and social stresses such as changing jobs, moving, divorce, etc. are frequently considered good subjects for biblio/poetry, e.g. the article by Cynthia Blomquist Gustavson, M.S.W., entitled "The Use of Poetry in Identifying and Coping with the Emotional Tasks of Moving" (JPT, Fall 1995, pp. 33-39).

I was especially interested in an article by John Graham-Pole (JPT, Spring 1996, pp. 129-141) entitled "Children, Truth, and Poetry". Dr. Graham-Pole is a pediatric oncologist. He discusses his own poetry as related to the children with cancer he has treated. Since I have written a number of poems regarding my own patients (see my book *Like the Trailings of a Comet on an Endless Journey*, Infinity Publishing.com, 2005) I can appreciate the emotion he has experienced. Thus biblio/poetry therapy can help the therapist as well as his patients.

The article, "Adverse Reaction to Poetry Therapy: A Case Report" by Ronald Pies (JPT, Spring 1993, pp. 143-147) describes a patient with personality and post traumatic stress disorders who became very distressed by exposure to certain poetic material. This might suggest a "down side" of biblio/poetry therapy but on the other hand this reaction could be used by the therapist to help expose the reason(s) the literary piece was so upsetting.

An important paper emphasizes that biblio/poetry therapy will be of most value if it is presented in the clients' own language (JPT, Fall 1994, pp. 3-14).

The use of poetic techniques is often helpful when writing poetry therapy. Thus simile, contrast, metaphor, rhyme, etc. can bring forth thoughts and descriptives which cannot be created in prose (Warren L. Morton, JPT, Summer 1996, pp. 217-226). Morton also cites Carl Jung's use of imagination as a technique in extending the meaning or intention of a poem to a higher and/or deeper levels of the mind or psyche.

An example of how biblio/poetry therapy can reorient one's image of himself or herself can be found in the Daniel U. Bowman, et. al. article entitled "Exploration of Sexual Identity through Poetry Therapy" (JPT, Fall 1996, pp. 19-26).

Psychoanalysts use poetic techniques by considering the analysant's "free thought." The analyst's goal is to interpret the analysant's words in search of an understanding of his or her mental illness. The goal is to assist the patient move forward toward self-understanding (Manya Beau, JPT, Spring 1997, pp. 137-141). Indeed, the dialogue between the analysant and analyst can indeed be considered "free verse".

In short just about every psychological, psychiatric, societal, familial, cultural and even many medical problems can be addressed to some extent through the medium of literary/poetic thought or interpretation.

In summary, biblio/poetry may be a representation of the communicative power of the spoken and written word. It can be used in individual or group settings. Biblio/poetry can extend its value by enjoining the total input from a wide variety of individual inputs from many different backgrounds. Likewise other creative arts (painting, sculpturing, acting, etc.) may have a similar therapeutic value. Physical activities such as dancing, exercising, engaging in sports, multifactorial activities such as yoga, and various forms of meditation and exercise also have therapeutic value by their ability to relax the mind sufficiently to allow self contemplation and understanding.

People who keep journals or diaries understand the value of the written word. They use their personal experiences as learning tools to help remember pleasant experiences, recall the names of valuable people they have encountered, record their successes and failures, and help them not to "make the same mistake twice".

Are spirituality and biblio-poetry therapy related? Certainly belief in a higher being is thought to be a stabilizing and comforting entity for many people. For many it seems to complement their lives and guides them in their life pursuits. Prayer and meditation can often suppress anxiety and irritability. Music also has therapeutic value, both when one listens to it, creates it, or plays a musical instrument. It has been said: "Music can calm the raging beast." Finally, consider how dancing can result in a feeling of happiness and euphoria.

In summary, biblio/poetry therapy can be a valuable therapeutic tool to help mitigate and even help cure many illnesses, especially those of the mind. It expands and transcends the acts of common speech and thought. It enters the door of contemplative thought processes allowing associations that lead to a deeper understanding of oneself and others. In short, reading, hearing and writing prose and/or poetry can be valuable in both sickness and in health.

PART III

HOW BIBLIO/POETRY THERAPY
CAN HELP HEAL THE ADDICTED

"Two roads diverged in a yellow wood
And sorry I could not travel both
And be one traveler, long I stood
And looked down on as far as I could
To where it bent in the undergrowth."
- Robert Frost

The above is an example of a portion of a poem by Robert Frost entitled, "The Road not Taken." It is an example of a possible poem suitable for discussion at a biblio/poetry therapeutic session. "Which road would you have taken?" The one that leads to a happy and productive life or the one that leads to false promises and self destruction?

Thus we arrive at the major goal of this book. How can biblio/poetry therapy help the addicted individual? Firstly, the addict has to admit and accept his or her illness and agree to do whatever is necessary to help him or her heal. Of course this includes individual psychotherapy, group therapy (AA or other similar gatherings), medication, and the support of friends and family.

Verbalization in a therapeutic environment with an afflicted addict allows him or her to express feelings such as frustration, loneliness, insecurity, depression, anxiety, self-hatred, hatred of others, etc. that led to the addiction in the first place.

Can everyone express himself or herself in writing? Can everyone appreciate the significance or meaning of a literary exposition? Probably not. Many people have a closed mind to such techniques. However, I happen to believe that when challenged almost anyone can open his or her mind to free thought. I recently conducted a seminar in poetry writing for an elderly group of people wherein I read some of my poems and then at the end of the session asked everyone (about 20 people many of whom have never written a poem) to write a poem in about 10 minutes. We then would vote (for first, second and third place) as to which were the best. The first place winner would receive a copy of my book *Like the Trailings of Comet on an Endless Journey*. Not surprisingly, the poems written by the attendees were very good!

Thus one approach to biblio-poetry therapy for the addicted would be to put down his or her thoughts, concerns, hurts, aches, etc. in some poetic or free-thinking style. The poems or writing do not need to contain rhyme or be organized. They can be organized later, perhaps after a rethinking or a discussion of the content. In an individual or group therapy environment poems or narratives can be analyzed, discussed, extended, or even challenged. This could lead to insight and understanding regarding the reason(s) the person has an addictive problem.

Mari Atschuler states that the addicted individual *can* be helped by reading and writing (JPT, Spring 2000, pp. 165-173). She cites the "12 step" programs as stepping stones for the verbalization of the individual's illness. Dr. Atschuler's paper is very instructive regarding how one goes about using biblio/poetry therapy as a therapeutic tool. She uses a number of techniques during therapy sessions with her patients. She suggests a variety of poetic exercises for them to try and then present them to the group for discussion. She teaches her clients three writing techniques to help them get started: 1. free (thought) writing; 2. clustering of ideas; and 3. the use of a "word basket" of poetry verses (similar to the magnets on which are written short phrases and put on some people's refrigerators) or word "cut ups" (phrases, or semi-complete sentences e.g., "If I could I would..."). Clients would be given the opportunity to read their writings to others in the group for discussion or simply pass them around for silent reading. Some boundaries are set with regard to what they are allowed to write in their poems so that the feelings of other members of the group are not be hurt by the words. One patient in such a setting commented, "I (now) understand that you can deal with your feelings and emotions in different ways". The program appeared to be very successful. She went on to state that "poetry therapy as a creative art modality is especially helpful in working with this population, in outpatient as well as residential settings". She further writes: "The people weave separate threads into a tapestry of no small light."

Alisha Howard studied the effects of external music and biblio/ poetry therapy on the ability of these methods to help clients perform "on-task" activities (JPT, Fall 1997, pp. 81-102). Her conclusion was that the exposure to these arts was "beneficial".

Wanda Springer (JPT, Vol. 19, No. 2, pp. 69-81) also explored the use of poetry in the therapy of clients recovering from addictions. She defines poetry as "a form of expressive language that uses metaphors and images to communicate meaning." Poetry does often employ a "metaphor" to communicate a meaning beyond the word or phrase. The word comes from the Greek word **meta** meaning "above or over" and **phorein**, meaning to carry from one place to another. Thus it means to go "beyond the word or phrase itself" (see also the Glossary).

She points out that the therapeutic use of poetry in psychiatry has many examples: The "free talking" used in Freudian psychoanalyses, therapeutic writing, aspects of Jungian psychology (evoking the images of the unconscious mind), existential psychiatry (using images that reflect a person's state of mind), and other techniques of psychotherapy.

Wanda Springer probably presents the best discussion regarding the value of poetry as a therapeutic tool. Questions that may be of value in the mind of the writer (or reader) of a poem are "What do I think of when I read this poem?" "What does it remind me of regarding my life?" "How do the words make me feel?" "Can the words help me to heal?" "Do they give me insights into my life (and why I turned to addictive behavior)?"

She also discusses the neuropsychology of brain function with regard to poetry. It is believed that the amygdala interprets sensory inputs from the thalamus and changes these inputs into emotional and hormonal signals. The left side of the brain is used for verbalization, writing, logic and rationalization. The hippocampus organizes and integrates information from the amygdala. Finally, the prefrontal cortex filters this information by associating it with pertinent prior knowledge and translates it into the spoken word.

Springer references Nicholas Mazza who published the book "Poetry Therapy: Theory and Practice (2003)." He defined poetry therapy as follows:

1. A "receptive/prescriptive" component which uses existing poems to "receive" messages of perception and how they might serve as a "prescription" for changing one's life;

2. An "expressive/creative" component which encourages the writing of a poem by a client to be delivered up to a group of therapists for evaluation and encourages them to provide feedback to the client; and

3. A symbolic/ceremonial component wherein the therapist "serves up" for discussion or interpretation poetic metaphors, stories, quotations, sayings, etc. attempting to find relevance in their meaning and how they relate to (individual) or the groups' illness(es) and life experiences.

Springer states that the addict often suffers from a lack of motivation and ambivalence. She believes that poetry writing can help resolve ambivalence of thought and action. She used Mazza's model of group therapy to develop an outpatient program for clients' recovery from addiction. She asked her group to compose a poem or poetic statement reflecting what being an addict is like (e.g. "being an addict is like…."). They came up with the following:

…"Feeling like crispy apples in my brain"

"Addiction is a dark dreary room and I am the caged bird inside"

"Wanting to get out to blue skies and freedom…"

"My addiction feels like I'm being lifted off the ground…"

Another technique used by Springer is the setting up of "poetry stations". Group members were invited to go to a poetry station where "poetic stems" were set up. The following are examples of a poetic "stems":

"If you knew me…"

"I am not happy when…"

"I keep on because…"

"I am happy when…"

"What matters most is…"

"My greatest strength is…"

Hundreds of other stems could be conceived.

However, Springer concluded by stating that poetry therapy is not for everyone. Some individuals are incapable of exploring the deeper aspects of their psyche. For those addicts poetry therapy will not be of value.

Hynes and Hynes-Berry (Biblio/Poetry Therapy The Interactive Process: A Handbook) (see section VIII, Further Reading) details the overall methodology of biblio/poetry therapy in great detail. They summarize these details as follows:

Firstly, they state the definition and components of biblio-poetry therapy. These include 1. The concept that it is interactive between the therapist and his or her client(s); 2. It can take place between the therapist and one client or be employed in a group therapy environment; 3. The purpose of it is to enhance self-esteem and lead to an understanding of one's illness that will result in improved social behavior; and 4. It requires a skilled therapist and an interactive client (or clients).

Secondly, the major goals of biblio-poetry therapy are to 1. Improve one's ability to recognize and react appropriately to one's own thoughts and feelings as well as those of others; 2. Open the door to self-understanding and an appreciation of the factors that brought on the mental illness; 3. Improve relationships with others leading to an awareness and understanding of the problems of others; and 4. Increasing one's ability to respond effectively to adversity by a greater understanding of the world around us.

Thirdly, the bibliotherapeutic process is described as follows: 1. It involves the understanding that bibliotherapy is only a "catalyst" or pathway to reality; it is not an end in itself; 2. It requires (concentrated) engagement of the reading or writing material put forth for discussion; 3. One must recognize his or her reactions to the bibliotherapy and attempt to apply these reactions to his or her illness; 4. One must be able to juxtapose his or herself into the crux of the bibliotherapeutic piece being presented such that it leads to self-understanding.

Fourthly, the bibliotherapeutic skills of the therapist are an important determinant of success (e.g., in his or her ability to select the right piece of literature for a given patient or group of patients). The material can be poetry, prose, audiovisual presentations produced by others or the poetry or prose written by the client or clients in a group. The latter has the value of more being more pertinent for an individual patient or group of patients.

Fifthly, the bibliotherapy must have certain qualities if it is to be effective. This includes 1. The ability of the therapist to understand and interpret a client's illness and how he or she is reacting to it; 2. The therapist must have a true empathy and respect for his or her client or clients; 3. The therapist must be mature, honest in his or her remarks, able to adapt to various emotions of the client or clients and be able to carry them forward to the goal of self-understanding; 4. The therapist must also be familiar with the various form of creative writing as well have good knowledge of pertinent literature; he or she must also have some creative writing skills regarding poetry and prose.

A typical session could go in many directions depending on the client or clients, their age, their problem, their skill in using biblio/therapy as a therapeutic process, etc. The therapist must be ready to present material for discussion. However, he or she should encourage input from the client or clients. The session should begin with an "open-ended remark" such as "do you (does anyone) have material to present (from the literature or personal writing)?" If no one comes forward the therapist should present his or her material. It is important to emphasize that the literature is only a tool; it is not something to criticize or praise in and of itself. The focus should always be "What is your response to the piece?" How does it relate to you?...To your mother or father, to someone in the group, etc." "How did you feel when you heard the poem read aloud?" How did it make you feel when you read it? Can you relate it to your addiction(s)?

Finally, in the end it is important to evaluate the client's benefit from his or her experience with bibliotherapy. The bibliotherapist needs to grade each individual relative to his or her strengths and weaknesses. The degree of participation in the bibliotherapeutic exercise will also be scored. (And of course a record of the benefit obtained from the experience(s) recorded.) The client should have an opportunity also to grade himself.

CONCLUSION

I have discussed biblio/poetry therapy as a therapeutic tool that may assist the addict break his or her habit(s). Many of these "habits" are extremely dangerous and self-destructive as discussed in my brief examples of various addictions. Many lead to helplessness, loneliness, anxiety, depression, as well as loss of income, criminal behavior, murder, suicide or death from the addictive element(s).

All forms of therapy must be used to conquer and cure the addict's illness, although no therapy will be of value if the addict does not have a strong desire and determination to rid himself or herself of the addiction(s). Biblio/poetry therapy may help to provide the insight to understand the etiology and dynamics of the addiction, learn to see oneself "as others see them" and rid themselves from the yoke of their addiction.

Therefore it is worthy of consideration in treating the thousands of individuals who have ruined their lives with one or more addictive habits.

GLOSSARY

Abstract language: Words that represent ideas, intangibles and concepts.

Addiction: An illness wherein one seeks perpetual internal satisfaction of the id (see below) through the habitual use of various psychoactive substances or activities. Breaking addictions can be difficult because it results in great psychological stress.

Analysand: A person undergoing psychoanalysis.

Archetype (Jungian psychology): An unconscious thought, or idea, or image derived from ancestors that is universally present in individual psyches.

Autism: An illness thought to be genetic wherein one tends to view life with respect to his or her own needs, ignoring objective reality.

Automatism: The state of independence or freedom of the will.

Automatic writing: Writing in which the writer does not pause but writes quickly.

Aware: Having knowledge; consciousness; cognizant.

Beta-endorphin: A neurotransmitter that modulates mood and pain.

Bibliotherapy: The use of written material to help ameliorate psychiatric illnesses. It can be offered by the therapist or written by the client.

Closure: The ending of a poem or other literature.

Constructivism (psych.): A formal organization of concept or thought.

Countertransference: In psychoanalysis, transference to the analysand on the part of the analyst regarding the repressed feelings aroused by the analysand.

Collaborative poetry: Poetry written by a group of people.

Cynicism: The state of believing that selfishness motivates human action, disbarring the motives of others even if they are humanistic.

Deconstruction (psych.): Diminishing or reducing a concept, thought or idea to allow examination of the parts.
Ego (psych.): Part of the psyche apparatus that experiences and reacts to the outside world; mediates between the id and the outside world.

Dopamine: A neurotransmitter that modulates mood and pain; also inhibits norepinephrine release.

Free verse: Poems that lack meter.

Gaba (short for gammaaminobutyric acid): A neurotransmitter that shuts down all other neurotransmitters.

Haiku: A Japanese style verse (can be in English or other languages); a poetic form of three lines containing seventeen syllables arranged 5-7-5.

Id (psych.): That part of the psyche that seeks satisfaction according to the pleasure principle; it is modified by the ego and superego. Addictions attempt to "oversatisfy" the id.

Image: A mental picture; a concrete representation of something or someone.

Integration (psych.): The organization of the constituent elements of an individual's personality into a coordinated whole.

Letter poem: A poem written in the form of a letter.

List poem: A poem that enumerates a series of things or thoughts.

Metaphor (meta = change; phor = statement): A comparison that likens two unlikely things that actually have something in common. The word comes from the Greek meaning "transfer" or "carry across". Thus metaphors "carry" one word to the other. Example: United Airlines advertisement: "Life is a journey; travel it well."

Meter: Rhythmic measure of a line of verse.

Muse: The spirit force or person that inspires one to create a poem or poetic narrative.

Neurolinguistic: The neurological aspects of language.

Norepinephrine: A natural stimulant that is released by stress.

Nucleus accumbens: The pleasure center of the brain; its transmitters are dopamine and beta-endorphin. It is stimulated by additive stimulants.

Opiates: Drugs known as endorphins and enkephalins that act like exogenous opium; also known as narcotics which cause euphoria and block pain receptors.

Personality: The viable (outward) aspect of one's character.

Personality disorder: A psychological disturbance of personality.

Play therapy (psych.): Using the characteristics of how a child plays with toys to aid in identifying a psychological or psychiatric illness.

Poem: A text or verbal composition which usually conveys an experience, emotion, or thought.

Poetry therapy: Using poetry to assist in healing an individual afflicted with a psychological, psychiatric illness or psychological disturbing medical illnesses. Addictions may result from psychological illness, social trends or accidentally, but once in place can be considered a psychiatric/psychological illness. So being biblio/poetry therapy may assist in understanding its cause.

Psychoanalysis: A treatment technique that uses conscious and unconscious psychological processes to treat mental illness.

Psychology: The science of the mind or of mental states and processes; the science of human nature and behavior.

Psychotechnology: Using various techniques to control or modify human behavior. Biblio/poetry therapy could be considered a form of psychotechnology.

Psychotherapy: Using psychological or mental techniques to assist in curing patients with mental illnesses.

Rhythm: The "melody" that is created when words are put together.

Riddle poem: A poem that hides the true meaning; some poems written by individuals who have participated in biblio/poetry therapy may have hidden meaning in their words.

Serendipity (psych.): Discovering the understanding of a patient's psychological disturbances incidentally or accidentally.

Satirical poem: A poem that ridicules one's own or another's feelings.

Soulspeak: Oral, communal forms of poetry that is directed toward the unconscious area of the brain.

Spirituality (psych.): Referring to the conscious, vital principles of man; that which animates the body and mediates between the physical and non-physical aspects of life; the incorporated non-tangible being of man.

Superego (psych.): The part of the mind that mediates between the ego and social ideals. It is partly conscious and partly unconscious.

Symbolism (from the Greek, "To throw together"): In poetry, an image that represents a specific meaning; sometime it represents the unconscious mind (compare with metaphor).

Synesthism: The physiological "crossing" of the senses.

Transference (psych.): Reproduction of emotions directed toward a person other than the one to whom they were originally directed.

Unconscious mind (psych.): Part of the mind entertaining psychic material of which the conscious mind is unaware.

FURTHER READING

1. Mari Alschuler: Treating Addictions Through Poetry Therapy, J. of Poetry Therapy, Vol. 13, No. 3, 2000.

2. Al-Anon's Twelve Steps and Twelve Traditions, 1985.

3. Dennis C. Daley: Kicking Addictive Habits Once and for All (A Relapse Prevention Guide), Jossey-Bass Publishers, 1991.

4. Lana Dodes, M.D.: The Heart of Addiction, Harper Collins Publisher, 2002.

5. John Drary: The Poetry Dictionary, Story Press, 1995.

6. John Fox: Poetic Medicine; The Healing Art of Poem-Making, 1997.

7. Charles Gant, M.D., PhD and Greg Lewis, PhD. End Your Addiction Now (The Proved Nutritional Supplement Program That Can Set You Free), Warner Books, 2002.

8. A James Giannini, M.D. Drug Abuse: A Family Guide to Detection, Treatment and Education, Health Information Press, 1999.

9. M. Goldfield and R. Lawer: The Use of Creative Writing in Young Adult Drug Abusers, New Physician 20: 449-457, 1971.

10. Arleen-McCarty Hynes and Mary Hynes-Berry: Biblio/Poetry Therapy (The Interactive Process: A Handbook), North Star Press, Inc. 1994.

11. Nicholas Mazza. Twenty Years of Scholarship in the <u>Journal of Poetry Therapy</u>: The Collected Abstracts (June 2008), Vol. 21, No. 2, pp. 63-133.

12. Nicholas Mazza. Poetry: A Therapeutic Tool in the Early Stages of Alcoholism Treatment, <u>Journal of Studies on Alcohol</u>, 40.1, 123-128, 1979.

13. Nicholas Mazza: Poetry Therapy: Therapy and Practice, 2003.

14. Wanda Springer: Poetry Therapy: A way to heal for trauma survivors and clients in recovery from addiction, <u>J. of Poetry Therapy</u> Vol. 19, No. 2, pp. 69-71.

15. The Random House Dictionary of the English Dictionary (The Unabridged Dictionary), Jess Stein, Editor in Chief and Lawrence Urdang, Management Editor, 1966 (for definitions).

Postscript

I Am Addicted...
(*A Proclamation for the Afflicted*)

I am addicted to the clear blue sky while sitting under a warm sun;

I am addicted to the splash of cold water on my face as I prepare to begin another day;

I am addicted to the sizzling sound of eggs frying in a pan;

I am addicted to the smell of fresh, plump strawberries;

I am addicted to the laughs of my children when I tell them a funny story;

I am addicted to the feeling of strength and accomplishment after a vigorous workout;

I am addicted to the aroma of flowers on a fine Spring day;

I am addicted to the sound of fine music as it titillates my brain;

I am addicted to reading the stories and poems of great writers and also reading stories to my children;

I am addicted to the hustle and bustle of life as I watch mankind work and play;

I am addicted to the joy of a walk in the park as I listen to the sounds of G-d's creatures;

I am addicted to the feel of a warm bed as I lay my head on a soft pillow;

I am addicted to my loved ones who have stood by me in my fall from grace;

I am addicted to a warm shower as it washes away my hurts and misgivings;

I am addicted to the many wonders of nature;

And I am addicted to the power of G-d as he springs me to my feet and gives me the strength to find the path to a healthy mind and body;

But I am NOT addicted to the false promises of mood altering drugs, destructive life styles, or other self-harming habits.

ONE DAY...

(A poem written by a father to an addicted son)

One day you will marvel at the many stars in the sky
and the beauty of the glow of a full moon,
and then fall asleep counting your blessings;

One day you will awaken to the tapping
of a robin on your window sill
and rise from bed with a smile on your face;

One day you will watch the sunrise
over the mountains, stretch,
and feel happy that your day
is about to begin;

One day you will walk down the street
with your head held high,
in a hurry to get to work,
but take the time to pet a poodle
about to pass you by;

One day when you arrive at work
you will be greeted with "good mornings"
and smiles from your co-workers
who will be happy to see you;

One day you will feel great satisfaction because you accomplished a
difficult task
in record time and were congratulated
by your boss who appreciates your
intelligence and skills;

One day you will sit proudly
at the graduations of your children and grandchildren

as they receive the honors they deserve,
knowing they're smart because you're smart;

Later you will dance at their weddings
with the woman you love
and who loves you
and receive congratulations from
your friends and family;

And you will look forward
to the birth of more grandchildren
to add to the others
whom you love and cherish so much;

And one day soon you will
stand tall in front of your mirror
and be proud of whom you see
and thank G-d for your creation.

Love....

www.ingramcontent.com/pod-product-compliance
Lightning Source LLC
Chambersburg PA
CBHW031230280526
45784CB00004B/1520